Mckaleigh Sofie Durrett

Afternoon Tea

illustrated by Antonia Pylaeva

A story written for my children.
Love always,
Mommy

Mckaleigh Sofie Durrett

Afternoon Tea

illustrated by Antonia Pylaeva

Dear reader, always remember that friendship is a glorious and splendid thing. It is something to be cherished. True friendship is hard to find, but here in Fern Forest, there are many wonderful and kind friends of all colors and shapes, with different feathers and furs.

Our story begins deep within Fern Forest, where two very different friends lived: A wiry old Scottish Goat and an Uppity British Rabbit. I shall introduce them as Sr. Gordon the Goat and Master Hippity Hoppity the Rabbit. Although these two had many differences, their friendship was true.

One sunny, summer afternoon, Hippity Hoppity took out his favorite owl feather pen and began to scratch a brief note in his rolling cursive handwriting. It read:

My Dearest Friend,
Tea for two, at my burrow.
Sincerely,
Hippity Hoppity

Hippity Hoppity, dipped his large gold signet ring that sat proudly upon his left paw into the hot red wax and then stamped the letter shut. He leaned out the window, handing the letter to Sparrow, the delivery bird. In the Rabbit's rather regal dialect, he thanked the bird and sent him on his way.

My Dearest
Friend
Tea for two,
at my burrow.

In a dusty small room, next to a crackling fire, sat Gordon. He was in a terrible mood, per usual. He huffed and he puffed as he took his long poker and rustled the embers in the hearth. The fire bubbled and crackled as if it were complaining along with the grumpy old Goat.

All of a sudden, a crash and a yelp indicated the arrival of Sparrow, the delivery bird. The bird was extremely clumsy.

Gordon rolled his eyes.

Peeling open the letter, he read it slowly. He was in no mood for a social call, but a lovely cup of tea did sound quite nice. So, he stood slowly, adjusted his loose-fitting kilt, and headed for the door.

As Gordon walked down the lane - more so limping, because last spring he had hurt his back - he came across Ray. Ray was always inviting himself places or trying to tag along and it drove Gordon nuts! To no surprise, Ray the squirrel, who didn't seem altogether mentally sane, began to ask where the old Goat was heading and if he could join.

Gordon gave him a look that could freeze a pond and in his gruff voice simply said, "Yer aff yer heid."

Dear reader, this is an old Scottish saying, and it is simply very rude and is not to be repeated around good company!

Gordon went on his way. Ray was left with his jaw on the ground in complete and total shock. But seconds later the ditzy squirrel couldn't remember why he was even standing in the middle of the path and scurried off for more nuts.

Meanwhile, Hippity Hoppity, who prided himself on presentation, was ironing his best linens, buffing his silver tea set, and mixing the batter for his hotcakes. He had left his glasses by his favorite book and squinted, looking for the rest of the ingredients. He added a sprinkling here and a dash there to the large bowl. The old kettle on the stove began to whistle and scream, notifying the sophisticated rabbit that the Dandelion Tea was ready.

The Rabbit was very particular when it came to presentation and etiquette, always pour the milk in first. To prevent the hot tea from cracking your delicate China cup, you must use your teaspoon and move it gently backwards and forwards to dissolve the sugar. He always did at least three big scoops. He loved anything lovely and sweet.

Dear reader, always, always remember, keep those pinkies down! It is just ghastly that this new trend of one's finger raised like a flagpole had become popular.

The door flung open, the wind slapping it hard against the wall, knocking a watercolor illustration of Hippity Hoppity's rather large family off the wall. Gordon limped inside, complaining already as he slouched down in a lovely, overstuffed chair and barked, "Where's the Scran? I'm famished."

Dear reader, please do remember this old Scottish Goat can sometimes be hard to understand. In this case he is talking about food! He was indeed always hungry.

Hippity Hoppity jumped to going on and on about how delighted he was for the company and how the hotcakes had come out just right! He carefully arranged a tea plate for Gordon and asked in his most drawn out, uppity accent, "Maybe two lovely BIG scoops of sugar today, Gordon? It's so lovely when one's tea is sweet."

"No sugar. I'll take it black!" Gordon gruffed.

Hippity Hoppity laughed a dancing little giggle as he handed Gordon his tea and proceeded to prepare his own plate. Although Rabbit's trousers had become a tad bit tight, he helped himself to four large scoops of sugar and two hotcakes with extra honey before sitting down beside the Old Wiry Goat, who smelled a tad bit ripe.

The two began to chat as they always did when they had afternoon tea together. And of course, Hippity Hoppity held most of the conversation, chatting so continuously that he had no time to sip his tea or eat his hotcakes. He gossiped and he laughed, he told about Mother Hen who had misplaced one of her chicks yesterday and how back in the day a large tree limb had landed on poor Ray the Squirrel and how that was probably the cause of the squirrel's scattered mind... he went on and on. Finally, he looked up and realized Gordon had fallen fast asleep!

The most horrendous, wheezing sound was coming from the old goat. It was getting louder and louder. Hippity Hoppity winced, as his grandmother's flower vase began to rattle whenever the snores escaped from the old Goat's mouth!

Poor Hippity Hoppity looked on in utter disbelief. After all of the years of tea together, never had Gordon been rude enough to fall asleep on him! The old Goat snored so loudly that one by one, all of Hippity Hoppity's picture frames began to fall from the walls, cracking and shattering as they hit the floor. The sound alone of breaking wood and shattering glass should have woken the Goat, but alas it did not! The Poor Rabbit watched in horror as his beautiful home fell apart!

The 100-year-old oak tree rattled, its leaves falling to the ground. The tree had been the proud home of Hippity Hoppity for many, many years, and the little red front door in the center of the thick trunk now shook! The birds that normally lived in the tall tree branches squawked and took off in fear. "Earthquake!" they shouted.

It was complete and total chaos. The other animals of Fern Forest came running. Giants hadn't lived in those parts in many years... had one returned? Come to terrorize them and take their homes?

Hippity Hoppity's neighbors gathered around the large oak tree.

Mother Hen scooped up all her little chicks beneath her warm feathers, in a protective motherly manner.

Mr. Toad waved his walking cane around, directing traffic and trying to demand attention, his old military days coming back as he took control of the situation.

Delilah Fox cried in fear, wrapping her feather boa tightly around her neck. She hadn't had time to do her hair that morning and was more concerned about her appearance than the fact that Giants had potentially come to terrorize them all. She was quite a vain creature.

Dear reader, remember Fern Forest is a community of neighbors of all different types with unique personalities and quirks. It most certainly takes all kinds to make the world go round.

Captain Badger, the leader of the Badger Patrol, directed his officers to surround the tree. One by one, the officers surrounded the tree trunk. Their black-and-white uniforms were ironed to a crisp.

"Come out with your arms up!" Captain Badger bellowed. He was not scared of a Giant, or whatever monstrous creature had taken Hippity Hoppity captive and was currently inside the burrow.

Poor Hippity Hoppity slowly exited his borough, cracking his red front door open ever so slightly as he creeped out. "Oh, my goodness," he spluttered. "I'm so sorry for all the commotion. It's just that my dear friend Gordon has fallen asleep! He's snoring, I can't seem to wake him. Oh, my goodness." He was completely mortified.

Detective Hedgehog stepped forward. " This is quite peculiar," he said, adjusting his old wire brim spectacles on the bridge of his long nose. "I shall come inside to investigate, and we will wake him up!"

Detective Hedgehog and Hippity Hoppity stepped inside. The noise coming from Gordon the Goat was deafening. Both animals had to place their paws over their ears. Gordon lay sprawled on the overstuffed chair. Crumbs from the hotcakes covered his kilt. Drool dripped from his mouth. Detective Hedgehog looked at Gordon and thought that it now made perfect sense why the old Goat had never married!

Hippity Hoppity was quite flustered. He kept explaining over and over again how this had never happened before. Every afternoon, they enjoyed tea together. Something must be wrong. Maybe there was construction going on at Gordon's pasture. Something that kept him up all night, and he was simply exhausted?

But Detective Hedgehog said he had not heard of any construction going on in Fern Forest. The detective began to poke around the room. He noticed the shiny buffed tea set... The crisp white linen on the dining table... The variety of tea cakes, hotcakes, and desserts... His long nose sniffed the dandelion tea and the many desserts. He slowly made his way into the kitchen. He adjusted his glasses, and finally after what seemed an eternity, he made a loud and a long " Ahhhahhhhh!"

Hippity Hoppity approached him, sliding on his glasses that he had found by his favorite book. "What have you discovered?" he asked curiously.

That is when, to Hippity Hoppity's horror, Detective Hedgehog presented him with the sleepy time potion. Dr. Bear had prescribed it to the Rabbit last fall when the Squirrel family had been rearranging their furniture. The poor rabbit couldn't get any sleep due to all the banging, knocking, and scraping from his upstairs neighbors.

Dear reader, you see, Mrs. Squirrel was an interior designer and was always coming up with new configurations for their little upstairs apartment. She was quite talented. To this day, the rabbit couldn't figure out how the squirrel had found six different locations for their grand piano in the teeny, tiny apartment.

All of a sudden Hippity Hoppity cried out, "Good gracious! I must've added the potion thinking it was the salt, into my hotcake batter!"

Dear reader, what a truly terrible mistake it had been for the Uppity Rabbit to make such a mistake. He felt deeply embarrassed as his whiskers shook and his cheeks turned crimson. But alas, we all do make mistakes, and forgiveness is all we can ask for!

Hippity Hoppity sat in a chair across from Gordon, wringing his paws in anticipation for the old goat to awake. He kept muttering to himself about what he should or shouldn't say to apologize to his dear friend. And finally, after what felt like eternity, the wiry old Goat awoke.

To the surprise of the quite anxious Rabbit, Gordon wasn't the least bit upset. "How lovely and comfortable this chair is by your fire, Hippity Hoppity, and the food was simply delicious," Gordon praised.

Before Hippity Hoppity could even respond, Gordon crossed the space between them and gave his friend a big, warm hug. "Lovely hospitality, as always, Hippity Hoppity," Gordon said with a smile. And he walked right out the door, not noticing a pile of broken pictures frames to his left, and headed for home, with a full belly and a grateful heart.

Dearest reader, Gordon was still a wee bit drowsy, I might add, but oh how he loved to nap, and he looked forward to his own chair by his very own fireplace.

That evening, Mr. Hedgehog sat down to a nice dinner with Mrs. Hedgehog, explaining his day, as he always did, at the end of a long day. He sat proudly after solving another case, with his many children gathered around him, asking lots of questions. Everyone was talking over each other in excitement.

While the sun began to set in Fern Forest, just down the lane, Sir Gordon the Goat stretched his arms into the air and took a deep sigh. Feeling quite refreshed from his long afternoon nap earlier that day, and his mid-afternoon nap he'd just awakened from, he lazily picked the rest of the hotcake crumbs off of his kilt, joyfully popping them into his mouth.

Just across the river, a creature wearing a black eye mask tiptoed into Delilah Fox's burrow and began to fill a large sack with her prize possessions. A robbery was taking place in Fern Forest...

But that, *dear reader*, is a story for another time,
when you revisit the Animals of Fern Forest
and all the wonderful creatures who dwell there
and the mischief they get up to!

The End

Milton Keynes UK
Ingram Content Group UK Ltd.
UKHW052234220524
443013UK00002B/30